Contents

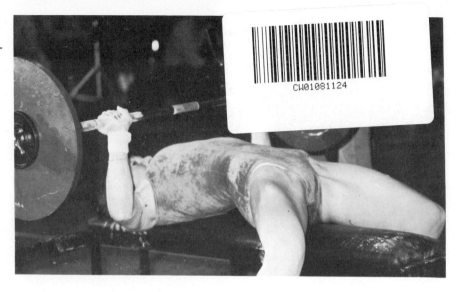

Photographs: left – Jarmo Virtanen's 295 kg squat; above – Rita Bass, bench press

Foreword

Since the foundation in 1973 of the International Powerlifting Federation, the number of participants has multiplied faster than could ever have been envisaged in the early years. It has gained acceptance and is practised extensively in most countries of the world.

Initially, powerlifting adopted the equipment and many of the rules already in use in Olympic style weight lifting. However, experience and constant monitoring at all levels has resulted in the emergence of specially designed equipment and of rules more appropriate to the different requirements of powerlifting. These are now universally accepted.

Today, powerlifting is recognised as a sport in its own right. It stands alongside weight lifting as one of the two principal strength lifting sports. The two disciplines complement each other and can justly be said to cater fully for the needs of anyone who finds that his or her sporting ambitions lie within the field of competitive lifting. National and

Milos Snajdr of Czechoslovakia dead lifts 372.5 kg

international powerlifting competitions cater for all age groups; it is a sport that can be successfully practised well into middle-age and beyond.

I am confident that this book, which covers all aspects of the sport, will be of great value and interest both to novices and to more advanced power lifters of all ages.

JOHN MOODY
Powerlifting Secretary, British Amateur Weight Lifters' Association

Introduction

Powerlifting started in the mid 1950s, in the U.S.A. and Britain. In those early days, the lifts were the curl, bench press and squat in that order. The rules were fairly lax and differed slightly between the two nations.

Around 1968, the curl was replaced by the dead lift and the order of competition was changed to that used today: squat, bench press and dead lift. The first of the World Team Championships took place in America in 1971, and they continued to be hosted by the U.S.A. until 1975 when they were held in England. At this time the competition rules were finalised and agreed, and the World Championships are now held all over the globe. With Eastern European countries beginning to compete, it can only be a matter of time before the sport is included in the Olympic Games.

If you wish to excel in the ultimate of strength participation, it will make great demands on you both mentally and physically. If you wish to compete, at whatever level, this book will explain the basics.

Equipment

Apparatus

All powerlifting apparatus is very expensive, but with care it will give a lifetime of service.

Barbell

All lifts are performed using a barbell made to specific dimensions with a sharply knurled gripping surface. The bar and retaining collars weigh 25 kg, and the round metal discs which are secured to each end range from a small 1.25 kg to the massive 50 kg.

Stands and bench

The platform must be flat, level and non-slip.

For the squat, a pair of stands is required. These should be adjustable in height and preferably hydraulically operated.

The bench used for the bench press must be flat and level with built-in adjustable stands to support the bar. Its length should be not less than 1.22 metres, width 29–32 cm and height 42–45 cm.

Referees' signals

A system of red and white lights will be used in competition to indicate whether the three referees consider this a good or failed lift.

Personal kit

During your competitive career you should strive to buy the best equipment you can afford. It is possible that you will use different kit for each of the three lifts. All personal equipment used in competition is subject to strict scrutiny by the referees and the rules are rigorously enforced. Keep it clean and in good repair or it will be rejected.

You must keep warm during training and competition and a good quality track suit will, therefore, be beneficial.

Footwear

Boots and shoes for the squat should be of a good quality leather with a flat, solid sole for good balance and a reasonable heel. You may also use these for the bench press, but you may need a slightly higher heel.

These days the best dead lifters use thin flat shoes, such as trampoline slippers, ballet pumps or karate shoes.

Heeled shoes for squat and bench press

Thin, flat shoes for dead lifting

Knee wraps

You will need at least two pairs of knee wraps, one for training and one for competition. These must be no more than 2 metres long and 8 cm wide. Learn how to put them on for maximum support. Wrist wraps may also be used, 1 metre by 8 cm maximum.

Belt

The maximum dimensions permitted are 10 cm wide and 13 mm thick. Big men should use the maximum size, but up to 75 kg competitors can get sufficent support from 10 mm thickness.

A wide belt is worn to support the back

Super suit

This you will certainly use for squatting and possibly for dead lifting. It is a very tight, leotard type of garment which you will need help to get on. It will be extremely tight on the legs, buttocks and over the shoulders and will give a lot of support. A much more comfortable costume is worn for the bench press.

A tee shirt is optional but if worn must be a proprietory brand and non-supportive. An athletic support must be worn but again it must not give assistance to the lifter. Swimming trunks are not permitted.

The super suit is tight and gives support

Safety

Pupils and competitors

Weight training, i.e. strength and muscle-building, is a very worthwhile end in itself. Strength assists in the development of skill acquisition, and is an important aspect of any physical fitness programme.

The sport of powerlifting requires great strength, speed, mental control, fitness and courage, as well as mastery of technique. Many of the world's greatest athletes employ progressive resistance principles in their training.

Weights, however, are impartial apparatus – they make no distinction between beginners and champions. Poor technique, reckless advancement of poundages or irresponsible behaviour can cause accidents. Listen to your coach or teacher. Apply the correct training principles, respect the limitations of each individual. Get your thinking right *before* you start to train. If you think and behave responsibly you will never hurt yourself or anybody else.

Always have a stand-in at each end of the bar

Consider the following:

(1) Confidence should not be confused with recklessness: the former is built on knowledge, the latter on ignorance. The only impression reckless weight training makes is on the floor.

(2) Although weight training and powerlifting are great fun because you can see and take pride in the progress you are making, to become an expert still takes time – time spent on understanding and mastering each step before moving on to the next. Don't try to run before you can walk.

(3) Before trying the next exercise or training plan, get and follow advice from your teacher or coach. Their job is to ensure that all the experiences you will have from the use of weights will be pleasant ones.

(4) Never train alone; always have one stand-in at each end of the bar. They should know what you are going to do and when.

To be ready for competition lifting, you must follow a sound training programme

Teachers and coaches

Every teacher wants to prevent accidents in physical education. Accident victims may suffer physical and psychological injury and distress with impaired future happiness. The P.E. programme may be cut back and all sorts of restrictions introduced. Teachers, coaches and authorities may also suffer stress and loss by being sued for negligence and damages if students are injured whilst using defective equipment; if there was inadequate supervision; if reasonable care was not exercised by the teacher.

To protect your pupils, your employers, your programme, your budget, YOURSELF – give full consideration to the recommendations set out below.

General physical education

(1) Have all equipment inspected regularly. Report in writing all deficiencies in apparatus, mats, floor surfaces, rigs, equipment, etc. to your superior. Do not use it until it is put right. Get the best equipment and keep it in good condition.

(5) Keep to your schedule of exercises. Do not advance poundages without your coach's advice. Do not sacrifice correct body position for poundage.

(6) Do not try to keep up with others who may seem to be making more rapid progress than yourself. Train at your own level and within your own capabilities. You will make progress.

(7) Horseplay and practical jokes can be very dangerous. If you are not getting enough fun out of serious powerlifting work, it's a poor programme.

(8) Check all apparatus before use and after each exercise. Check collars: ensure they are firmly secured. Make sure all bars are evenly loaded. Concentrate and be safety conscious.

(9) To be ready for competition lifting, you must follow a sound training programme. Technique must be mastered. Strength and power must be developed steadily. Your success in competition will depend upon a controlled and progressive approach to training.

(2) Make sure you have taught all the necessary skills, including safety procedures, before requiring students to exercise them in game, class or competition situations.

(3) Get medical approval before putting an injured student back into game, class or competition activity. Get and follow medical advice.

(4) Beginners need special teaching and supervision. A champion trying out an entirely new skill is a beginner at that skill. Supervision means being there when needed.

(5) Fatigue often precedes accidents. Students must be fit, at the time, for the work to be attempted. A tired pupil is often accident prone.

Weight training and powerlifting

In addition to the above, keep the apparatus locked up unless at least THREE people want to use it.

(1) Ensure that your layout for the different exercises in the weight training area is carefully planned. Barbells should not be too close to each other. Use mats under the weights. Transport of equipment requires great care. Do not permit horseplay.

(2) Check barbells, stands, benches, dumb-bells, etc. carefully before use. Make sure all collars are tight and barbells evenly loaded. Check each time apparatus comes out and after every set.

(3) Only train in an area where the floor is even, firm and non-slip. Do not permit pupils to train in bare feet. Balance in progressive resistance training is very important.

(4) Check and service the equipment regularly. It is very good insurance.

(5) Know why and when to teach specific exercises, as well as how. Good intentions are no excuse for ignorance. Attend an official coaching course.

(6) Make sure that stand-ins (two) are used for all exercises – one each side of the barbell ready to assist. Teach all pupils how to stand-in and catch. See that stand-ins know when and how to help.

(7) Ensure that pupil does not attempt limit poundages too soon. Too great a weight = bad body position = accident.

(8) Teach exercises carefully. Ensure strict exercise principles are employed at all times. Every pupil must advance at his own level.

(9) Use only token resistance during exercise learning phase. When muscle groups are weak they lack control. Lack of muscular control can lead to injury. Proceed with caution and always with careful supervision.

(10) Correct breathing on all lifts must be taught. Apply correct training principles.

(11) Encourage the use of firm shoes and warm clothing to train in, and fast training procedure to avoid 'local chilling' of muscles.

(12) Before driving your pupils to advanced training schedules or too early competitions, get your motives clear. Unless the well-being and safety of the performers comes above personal vanity and ambition it could be a dangerous programme.

(13) Display this advice in the gymnasium and ensure all students are familiar with the recommendations. Have your rules and enforce them. Stay in charge.

The lifts

1. Squat, stage 1 – bar is lifted from stands

2. Lifter has stepped back from stands

Squat

1 The bar is taken from the stands to rest across the shoulders (photo. 1). Head up, chest high.

The lifter steps back from the stands, feet approximately hip width apart. Feel the weight evenly over the feet, a well balanced strong position (photo. 2).

3. Stage 2

4. Stage 3

2 Taking a deep breath and maintaining a high chest, the lifter lowers the body by bending the legs (photo. 3).

3 The lifter lowers to the position required by the rules (photo. 4).

4 The lifter must now drive upwards to the erect position. This will demand great determination. Keep the knees turned outwards. Keep the head back, looking upwards.

5. Bench press, stage 1 – high arch to assist chest muscles

6. Bench press, stage 2

Bench press

1 The lifter must position the body on the bench as shown in photo. 5. This high arch enables the muscles of the chest to act in a much more effective pressing position.

2 The bar is taken from the stands (photo. 6) with the aid of assistants.

3 The bar is now lowered to the chest under control. When the bar rests on the chest, quite still, the signal will be given to press (photo. 7).

10

7. Stage 3

8. Stage 4

4 On the signal, the lifter must drive the bar from the chest with great determination. The head, shoulders and buttocks must remain in contact with the bench at all times. The feet must remain on the floor (photo. 8).

5 At the conclusion of the press, the referee will signal the completion of the lift and the loaders will return the bar to the racks.

Dead lift

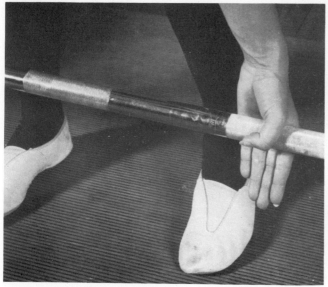

9. A strong grip for the dead lift – place thumb along bar

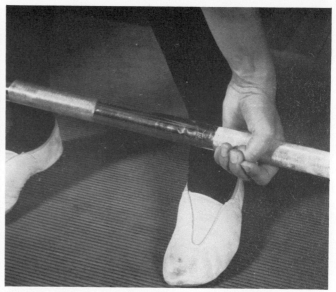

10. Wrap the fingers around it tightly to form hook grip

The grip

The grip on the bar is of vital importance. Here the hook grip is illustrated.

Place the thumb along the bar and wrap the fingers around it tightly, squeezing it against the bar (photos 9 and 10).

In addition, the lifter must use the 'alternate' gripping method, in which one hand faces forwards and the other backwards. This prevents the bar from rolling in the hands and so the grip remains secure.

11. Conventional style dead lift, stage 1

12. Stage 2

Conventional style of dead lift

1 Feet are placed under the bar, approximately hip width apart. The lifter grips the bar as described previously. The back is flat and strongly braced (photo. 11).

2 The lifter drives strongly with the legs, fighting to keep the back strong and flat. This requires great determination (photo. 12).

13. Conventional style dead lift, stage 3

14. Stage 4

3 As the bar passes the mid thigh, great resistance is thrown on the hip and back muscles as they pull the body to an erect position. The lifter must not 'lay back' against the resistance (photo. 13).

4 In the finishing position, the knees are locked and the head held up, chest high and shoulders braced (photo. 14).

Sumo style dead lift

Lifters with great leg and hip strength may favour this style.

1 The feet are placed very wide so that the shins are nearly vertical. The grip is narrow and between the legs, but otherwise as the grip described earlier (photos 15 and 16).

15. Sumo style dead lift – grip

16. Sumo style dead lift, stage 1

2 The lifter drives very strongly with the legs. Since the body is upright, the resistance is very much on the legs with the back having only a limited sharing effect on the load (photo. 17).

Knee height is a common 'sticking point'.

3 The lifter must be very determined in achieving upright position at the conclusion of the lift.

Because the grip is narrow, the lifter may find some difficulty in bracing the shoulders back at the completion of the lift (photo. 18).

17. Sumo style dead lift, stage 2

18. Stage 3

Competition procedure

Sumo style dead lift by Nanda, Indonesia

Powerlifting competitions are conducted in bodyweight classes. For men, there are eleven classes: up to 52 kg, 56 kg, 60 kg, 67.5 kg, 75 kg, 82.5 kg, 90 kg, 100 kg, 110 kg and 125 kg, and over 125 kg. Women have ten classes: up to 44 kg, 48 kg, as men up to 90 kg, and over 90 kg. Competitors will be weighed in two hours before the start of the competition.

Every competitor will have three attempts at each lift. Any lateral movement of the feet during these lifts will be cause for disqualification. The best of the successful attempts will be added together for a total score, and in each class the lifter with the highest total will be the winner.

Three referees will adjudicate all lifts and be responsible for the competition.

The weigh-in

You will be notified of the exact time of the weigh-in. Do not be late. Lifters are called in to the weigh-in room in order of the draw by the referees. If you are not present, you lose your turn and have to wait until the end, thereby cutting the time available to reduce your body weight, should it be necessary, and possibly shortening your preparation time.

Once inside the weigh-in room you are weighed naked. Only if you are overweight for your class will you be recalled to the scales. You are also required to give your starting weights for each of the three lifts, although these can be changed before the start of the competition.

Next, all your competition kit is checked by one of the referees. Anything you are going to use must be examined and stamped.

After this you should go to the platform, get your correct height for the squat racks and make sure the platform manager writes it down against your name.

If you have had to restrict your diet to make your bodyweight class, as most lifters do, you will probably need something to eat and drink. Do not gorge yourself; something light and fruit juice should be sufficient.

If all has gone to plan you should now have time to change into your kit and start your warm-up. You, or your coach, should check the scoreboard to see how many attempts will be taken before you are called to the platform, and adjust your warm-up accordingly.

Lift technique

Squat

Once the bar has been correctly loaded and your name called, you have exactly one minute to commence the lift. If you exceed this time, you forfeit the attempt.

You should be prepared for the squat, suit straps up over the shoulders, knee and wrist wraps on, and belt tightened.

If you require chalk on your shoulders, the coach can attend to this now.

Approach the bar from the rear and place your hands a comfortable distance apart. The hands may not be put on the inside collars or discs. Feet should be placed hip width apart. Ducking your head under the bar, you should endeavour to get the bar as far down your back as the rules permit: the top of the bar should not be more than 3 cm below the top of the anterior deltoid.

From this position, stand erect to clear the bar from the racks. Two short paces backwards should bring you quickly to the starting position: feet a comfortable distance apart but generally wider than hip width, knees straight, trunk erect and head up. You must wait motionless in this position for the referees' signal to commence: a downward movement of the arm and the verbal command 'squat'.

You must now bend the knees and lower the body with perfect control, and keep the combined weight of the bar and body directly over the centre of the feet. Any undue forward or backward movement will make you lose balance and place an undue strain on back or legs. As you descend, the trunk will incline forward, so maintain a tight upper body and do not allow the back to round. The belt will help you to do this.

When you reach the full squat (i.e. the top surface of the legs at the hip joint is below the top of the knees) stop the descent and drive vigorously upwards. Keeping the head up and elbows back will help to keep the trunk flat.

Squat by Tony Stevens, 100 kg world champion

18

At about 30° flexion you will experience a 'sticking point', but this can be overcome by keeping the knees out and driving the hips forward under the bar. Great determination must be used to get through this 'sticking point' but, once through, you should find it reasonably easy to reach the final erect position with legs straight. You are not permitted to move the bar on the shoulders, move the hands on the bar or move the feet so the correct starting position is vital.

The loaders may assist you to replace the bar on the racks after the signal.

Bench press

The apparatus must be placed in such a way that the competitor's head faces the front of the platform.

You must lie supine on the bench, and throughout the lift your head, shoulders and buttocks must remain in contact with the bench. Draw your feet back as far as possible, keeping them flat on the floor. They must not make contact with any part of the bench.

Now you must endeavour to get the buttocks as close to the shoulders as you can, to form a very high arch. A flexible spine is an advantage.

Bench press by Arthur White, 110 kg European champion

The last action is to grasp the bar. The maximum permitted distance between the forefingers is 81 cm and if you are comparatively strong in the pectoral muscles of the chest, this will be your hand spacing. If you are stronger in the shoulders and arms, you will take a much narrower grip.

The bar is handed to you at arm's length by the loaders, and from this position you must lower the bar to the chest. This lowering must be carefully

19

controlled, not so slow that it wastes a lot of energy but not dropped on to the chest. The bar must rest on the chest until you receive the referee's signal. You are permitted to sink the bar deep into the chest as long as it is done before the referee's signal. Many lifts are failed when this is done after the signal.

Now you must explode the bar off the chest without stopping or uneven extension until it comes to rest at arm's length. The hardest part of the lift, the sticking point, is usually experienced some 10 cm off the chest. It is at this point that one group of muscles takes over the work of another. These muscles are the anterior deltoid, pectorals and triceps, and assistance exercises must be used to strengthen these muscles as well as the whole shoulder girdle.

When the bar reaches arm's length, the referee signals the completion and the loaders replace the bar on the racks.

Dead lift

Often described as the king of the power-lifts, the dead lift is where competitions can be won or lost. No special equipment is required, just the bar and lifter.

Linda Miller of Australia's 212.5 kg dead lift

20

The bar must be gripped with both hands and lifted with one continuous movement until you are standing erect, with knees straight and shoulders back. The two basic styles, conventional and Sumo, are described on pp. 12–16.

A weak grip or small hands can reduce your chances of holding onto heavy dead lifts. The former is curable, the other is not. The hook grip is one answer to the problem. This is where the thumb is placed along the bar and the fingers wrapped around it. It is an excellent grip, but initially very painful.

The first problem is to get the bar moving off the floor. You have to overcome inertia with all the musculature relaxed; it is an absolutely 'dead' weight. This is not helped if you lack back and leg strength. Knee height is a common sticking point. If the bar is out of line it will leave you in an unbalanced position and make it difficult for the legs and back to do their work.

Failure to complete the lift and stand erect is often due to weakness in the upper back. To counteract this, lifters will often lean back, bend the knees and rest the bar on the thighs, all causes for disqualification.

Sumo style dead lift by Ed Cohen, USA

21

Assistance exercises

As well as performing the competition lifts, you will need to employ some assistance exercises to improve your power. Here are some that you might try, with the help of your teacher or coach. Many are shown in *KTG Weight Training* and *KTG Weight Lifting*.

Squat

Front squat

This is performed with the bar across the front of the shoulders. You will not be able to use as much weight as you can in the back squat.

Half squat

The bar is positioned exactly as for the back squat. Descend only half way to the full squat position, check, and then drive back to the erect position.

With weights in excess of your best squat, perform 5 sets of 3–5 repetitions to improve your confidence and develop tremendous power.

Bench press

The main muscles used in this exercise are the triceps, deltoid and pectoral, so any exercise that strengthens these will be an advantage. For example, straight arm pullover, bent arm pullover and front raises may be used. These exercises can be done as 5 sets of 3–5 repetitions.

Wide and narrow grip variations

The very wide grip (wider than competition position) throws the resistance on the pectorals.

With a narrow grip (no wider than shoulder width) and the elbows kept in, most of the work is done by the triceps and front deltoids.

Inclined bench press

With the angle of the bench at 45°, the bar is lowered from arm's length to chest and return. Again, use a variation in your grip.

This exercise can also be performed with dumb-bells. It can be made much harder if the feet are unsupported.

Press on back

Lie supine on the floor and have an assistant lift the bar to arm's length. From this position, lower the bar until the elbows and upper arms are resting on the floor. Pause, and then drive vigorously back to arm's length.

This exercise will help you to overcome the sticking point which is experienced when the bar is approximately 10 cm above the chest.

Dead lift

Straight-legged dead lift, bent forward rowing and trunk forward bends are valuable exercises. Because these movements are performed with relatively straight legs, 3 sets of 5–8 reps should be done.

Dead lift on blocks

The performer stands on an 8 cm platform to dead lift, 5 sets of 3 reps. This develops power from the floor.

Dead lift off blocks

The bar is supported on blocks at about knee height. Keeping the back almost vertical, pull to upright position, 5 sets of 3 reps. Sumo style may be used.

This is good for those with a poor finish.

Abdominals

The importance of abdominal exercises cannot be too greatly emphasised, and they must be included in every work out. They must be a planned and integral part of the training programme and not relegated to the end of the session as an afterthought or regarded as a nuisance. To neglect them is to invite competition failure.

Sit-ups and dumb-bell side bends are examples of abdominal exercises.

Dumb-bell side bend

Training

Objectives

Strength

The development of strength is dependent on overcoming great resistance through the muscular system. This will involve handling progressively heavier weights, and the training programme and exercises are arranged with this end in view.

Speed

Speed is dependent to a great degree on muscular strength to activate the joints against the resistance in the shortest possible time. Even though the heavy resistances handled in powerlifting reduce the speed of movement, lifters must harness all their mental powers to 'get the weight moving as fast as possible'.

Power

Power is the end-product of strength and speed. A very strong person can be slow in movement, and a very fast person comparatively weak in the powerlifting sense, but the successful powerlifter must develop great power. This means becoming strong *and* fast moving.

Courage

There is no doubt that the successful powerlifter must be 'brave' in the face of the maximum poundages that may have to be attempted to win a competition or set new records. This quality is best developed through successful training and the knowledge that all the necessary qualities of strength, speed, fitness and mastery of techniques have been thoroughly covered.

Fitness

Whatever physical activity you are involved in, be it running or swimming, major games, indoor activities or weight lifting, the greater the degree of basic physical fitness that can be developed and maintained, the greater the possibility of success in the activity. The powerlifter does not require the endurance fitness of the long-distance runner, but the systems of the heart, lungs and circulation must be highly efficient to ensure that he can train hard and recover quickly. Much of this fitness work will include speed work and flexibility training. This will involve short sprinting, standing high- and long-jumps, and simple gymnastic exercises to ensure full range of mobility in all the joint complexes. This, coupled with the normal powerlifting training, should ensure a standard of physical fitness which will help to bring the lifter to a high level of performance.

Methods – novices

The main objective is the progressive development of power, although there is also some small skill element attached to the three power lifts. We do not, therefore, have to devise and practise specific skill exercises.

Jenny Hunter, 56 kg European champion – dead lift

Warming up

Probably the most neglected part of any form of training with weights is the warm-up. This is important, especially for beginners who may well be weak, stiff, unfit, uncoordinated and inactive.

The warm-up should cover all the musculature and joints. Exercises that may be incorporated in the warm-up include: arms circling backwards, alternate arms swinging upwards, arms raising sideways and upwards, trunk circling, trunk bending forward, side bending, alternate toe touching with feet astride, good morning exercise, prone lying – head and shoulders raising or legs raising, astride jumping, skip jumping to crouch, lunges, squats, sit-ups, V-sits, short sprints.

Later this can form part of the fitness training programme.

Training schedule

Monday, Wednesday and Friday have always been popular training days for weight lifters and this seems ideal for the novice powerlifter. It allows the athlete to work hard and follow this with a day's rest and recovery.

Exercise	Sets	Reps
(Monday, Wednesday)		
High pull	3	8
Upright rowing	3	8
Back squat	6	8
Press on bench	6	8
Press behind neck	3	8
Triceps stretch	3	8
Sit-up	3	10–15
(Friday)		
Power clean	3	8
Front squat	6	8
Dead lift	6	8
Shrug	3	8
Seated incline dumb-bell press	3	8
Hyperextension	3	8
Dumb-bell side bend	3	10

Firm shoes and warm clothing should be worn.

Make sure that good body positions are maintained, and never sacrifice technique for extra weight.

Do not be too anxious to increase poundages in the early stages and make sure that each repetition is done in good style.

Between 15 and 18 days before the first competition the lifter should have a maximum try-out and use the best poundages as a guide for the second attempt in the competition. For example, if the best squat in the try out is 150 kg, you should aim at this for the second competition attempt.

Advanced lifters

When the lifter is ready to move on to a more advanced stage of training, there will be a reduction in the number of repetitions performed in each set and an increase in poundages and sets. He will start to specialise and concentrate on specific exercises to overcome individual weaknesses.

Planning is now more important and the coach will no longer be able to train athletes on a block principle. He needs to know each lifter thoroughly and to understand all the individual's mental and physical needs.

An additional training session can be introduced and it would seem that Sunday morning would be an appropriate time. This could be a fitness training or games training period or, nearer competition time, an additional power training session.

It is not necessary to divide lifters into intermediate and advanced ability groups. Once the basics have been learnt, training for all powerlifters can go along similar lines. The only difference will be in the sporting calendar, e.g. some lifters will be making divisional championships their objective, whilst others may be aiming at national or even world championships.

The training cycle for the powerlifter for each major competition may be broadly divided into two phases, preparation phase and competition phase.

Right – upright rowing
Far right – front squat

◀ Power clean

1 Preparation phase

The length of this phase will depend on the number of major competitions the lifter is preparing for. The national squad lifter, for example, will probably compete three times a year, at his divisional championships, the nationals and hopefully the world; whereas a lifter of lesser ability may only compete twice, at county and divisional levels. It is unlikely ever to exceed 12 weeks and in most cases will be 8–10 weeks.

Body-building exercises play a major part at this stage, some fitness and endurance training should also be done. There should be no emphasis on the competition lifts, but assistance exercises such as narrow stance squats, narrow grip bench presses and straight legged dead lift would be incorporated.

This period would take up to within eight weeks of the competition and the body weight would be at approximately competition weight.

Exercises should be performed fast and rest periods between sets should be cut to a minimum, to increase muscular endurance.

Exercise	Sets	Reps
(Monday)		
Upright rowing	3	8
Press behind neck	3	8
Narrow stance squat	5	6–8
Seated incline dumb-bell press	5	6–8
Shrug	3	8
Screw curl	3	8
Bent leg sit-up	5	20
(Wednesday)		
Power clean	3	8
Bent over rowing	3	8
Narrow grip bench press	5	8
Front squat	5	8
Round back good morning	3	8
Triceps exercise	3	8
Dumb-bell side bend	3	10
(Friday)		
High pull	3	8
Bent arm pullover	3	8
Leg press	3	8
Leg curl	3	8
Straight leg dead-lift	4	6–8
Bench press	3	8
Hyperextension	5	8–10

2 Competition phase

Exercise (Monday or day 1)	Sets	Reps
Squat (competition stance)	2	5
Knee wraps	2	3
Knee wraps	2	2
Bench press (competition position)	3	3
	2	2
	3	1
Dead lift	1	5
	1	3
Straps	3	1
Abdominal work, and stretching exercises		

Exercise (Friday or day 3)	Sets	Reps
Squat (competition stance)	1	5
	1	3
	2	2
	3	1
Bench press (competition position)	1	5
	2	3
	2	2
Dead lift	1	6
	1	4
	2	3
Abdominal work		

(Wednesday or day 2)	Sets	Reps
Power clean	3	3
Triceps exercise	3	5
Round back good morning	3	5
Seated incline dumb-bell press	3	5
Press behind neck	1	5
	2	3
Abdominal work		

(Sunday or day 4)

If the fourth training session is included each week, it should take the form of day 2, or alternatively it can be used for specific exercises such as grip work and short range power movements, i.e. half squat, dead lift from boxes and dead lift standing on blocks.

The intensity of the work-outs can now be stepped up and more emphasis be placed on the competition power lifts, together with really heavy body-building work. One would expect the body weight to increase 3–5% above competition body weight, and remain that high until approximately seven days before the competition.

Fitness training can be reduced and repetitions drastically cut, and particular attention paid to technique on the three lifts. The three power lifts must be the core of the programme.

The final seven days before a competition can best be described as an active rest period. Some lifters like a full seven days break from the weights but as a general rule the lighter competitors tend to take less rest than those who are heavier. Indeed, it is not unknown for some lifters to work right up to the day of the competition.

After a competition, many power-lifters take a partial or even total break from training, but this is up to the individual.

Conclusion

Train under the strict supervision of a qualified and experienced coach. Do not be put off by the well-meaning, would-be coach who is likely to give you dangerous and incorrect information. Good coaches are difficult to find but they are around and they will possess a B.A.W.L.A. qualification which is recognised worldwide.

You are an individual with your own strengths and weaknesses. In consultation with your coach, discover exactly what these are and discuss how best to overcome them. If you are determined and dedicated and prepared to apply yourself to often painful, frustrating and rigorous training programmes, you can get a lot of enjoyment and success in this wonderful sport of powerlifting.

B.A.W.L.A.

Weight lifting awards

The schools weight lifting awards scheme is designed as a progressive incentive for pupils starting weight training and eventually moving on to weight lifting. The examiner for all three grades is the pupil's normal teacher or coach. Certificates for all grades are free.

All pupils participating in these award schemes should be members of the B.A.W.L.A. Badges and certificates can be obtained from the officials of the Schools Association.

Full details of these and teacher awards can be obtained from the B.A.W.L.A. Coaching Secretary.

Lars Noren of Sweden – squat

Coaching scheme

The Association maintains a National Coaching Scheme with a National Coach assisted by Staff Coaches, Senior Coaches, B.A.W.L.A. Coaches and B.A.W.L.A. Instructors and holders of the School Teachers Award and the B.A.W.L.A. Leaders Award.

This scheme is under the control of the Coaching Committee which is responsible to the Central Council of the Association for all matters concerning the provision of qualified coaches and instructors and the raising of the standard of weight lifting and weight training.

Coaching grades

(a) Holders of B.A.W.L.A. Leaders Award: Recognised as capable of giving basic instruction in weight training and elementary weight lifting.

(b) Holders of School Teachers Award: Recognised as capable of giving elementary instruction in weight training for children of school age only, and of passing children for the awards of the Schools Weight Lifting Association or the Schools Weight Lifting Scheme of the B.A.W.L.A.

(c) B.A.W.L.A. Instructor: Recognised as capable of performing the duties of the holders of the School Teachers Award plus giving elementary instruction in weight lifting, powerlifting and weight training to all age groups.

(d) B.A.W.L.A. Coaches: Recognised as capable of instructing all types of weight training, weight lifting and power-lifting, and of assistance at the practical part of courses for Instructors.

(e) B.A.W.L.A. Senior Coaches: Recognised as fully competent to assist on courses for coaches and instructors and to organise, take courses and complete examinations for the School Teachers Weight Training Award and B.A.W.L.A. Leaders Award.

(f) B.A.W.L.A. Staff Coaches: Recognised as fully competent to set, mark and assess examination papers at the discretion of the Coaching Committee.

Overseas readers may contact one of the B.A.W.L.A. officials for local details.

Important addresses

B.A.W.L.A. General Secretary and Coaching Secretary:
W.W.R. Holland O.B.E.
3 Iffley Turn, Oxford.

B.A.W.L.A. Powerlifting Secretary:
John Moody,
15 Byron Close, Stevenage, Herts.

B.A.W.L.A. Coach responsible for powerlifting: G. Leggett,
'Hideaway', 19 Lowestoft Road,
Carlton Colville, Lowestoft, Suffolk.

B.A.W.L.A. Director of Coaching:
P.J. Lear,
The Willows, 4 Ford's Heath,
Shrewsbury, Shropshire.

Photographs

Cover, showing Tony Stevens, by Lee Jackson; inside front cover, pp.1, 2, 5, 6, 17, 18, 19, 20, 21, 25, 31 and inside back cover, courtesy of *International Powerlifter* magazine; all other photographs by Trevor Clifford – with thanks to Lorraine Dansie and Gary Taylor for demonstrating the lifts.

Index